ARMORED VEHICLES

Valerie Bodden

CREATIVE ✦ EDUCATION

Published by Creative Education
P.O. Box 227, Mankato, Minnesota 56002
Creative Education is an imprint of The Creative Company
www.thecreativecompany.us

Design and production by Liddy Walseth
Art direction by Rita Marshall
Printed by Corporate Graphics in the United States of America

Photographs by DefenseImagery (Sgt. Brandon D. Bolick, Pvt DeAngelo Wells, Staff Sgt. William Tremblay), Getty Images (Ed Darack, Karen Kasmuauski, Louie Psihoyos, Stocktrek Images, Chung Sung-Jun, U.S. Department of Defense), iStockphoto (Breckeni, Craig DeBourbon, Anton Ferreira, Nicholas Homrich, Philip Lange, Narvikk, NickyBlade), Sakini

Library of Congress Cataloging-in-Publication Data

Bodden, Valerie.
Armored vehicles / by Valerie Bodden.
p. cm. — (Built for battle)
Includes bibliographical references and index.
Summary: A fundamental exploration of armored vehicles, including their speed and carrying capacity, history of development, armor and other features, and famous models from around the world.
ISBN 978-1-60818-123-0
1. Armored vehicles, Military—Juvenile literature. I. Title.
UG446.5.B59 2012
623.7'475—dc22   2010053674

CPSIA: 030111 PO1447

First edition
2 4 6 8 9 7 5 3 1

BUILT for BATTLE

ARMORED VEHICLES

Valerie Bodden

TABLE OF
contents

5. What Is an Armored Vehicle?

9. Early Armored Vehicles

13. Sizes and Parts

17. Armor and Windows

19. Armored Vehicle Crews

21. Armored Vehicles in Battle

FAMOUS ARMORED VEHICLES

10. Sd Kfz 251

16. Humvee

23. Stryker

24. Glossary

24. Index

24. Web Sites

24. Read More

Bullets fly through the air.

They hit a huge truck but bounce off its side.

The truck keeps moving over the rough ground.

It comes to a river and drives right through it!

This is an armored vehicle!

Armored vehicles are cars, trucks, or tanks that are covered with ARMOR. Armored vehicles move TROOPS or supplies from one place to another. Some are used as ambulances. Most armored vehicles drive at speeds of 30 to 70 miles (48-113 km) per hour.

Soldiers using an armored vehicle as they train for battle

An armored vehicle that was used in World War I (1914–1918)

Armored vehicles were first used in battle around 1914. They were cars or trucks that had extra metal attached around the outside. Later, special vehicles with armor were built.

★ Famous Armored Vehicle ★
Sd Kfz 251

COUNTRY

Germany

ENTERED SERVICE

1939

LENGTH

19 feet (5.8 m)

WIDTH

6.8 feet (2.1 m)

WEIGHT

8.7 tons (7.9 t)

FASTEST SPEED

33 miles (53 km) per hour

CREW

2 (plus 10 passengers)

The Sd Kfz 251 carried troops next to fast-moving German tanks. It had wheels in the front and TRACKS in the back to help it drive easily over rough ground.

Some armored vehicles look like the trucks that drive on the highway. Others look like big, boxy tanks. They can be 15 to 30 feet (4.6-9 m) long and 8 to 10 feet (2.4-3 m) wide.

Most armored vehicles are tan or green.

This makes them blend in with sand or trees.

Some armored vehicles have wheels.

Others move on tracks.

These green armored

vehicles in Japan

move on tracks

Humvee

COUNTRY

United States

ENTERED SERVICE

1985

LENGTH

16.3 feet (5 m)

WIDTH

7.6 feet (2.3 m)

WEIGHT

6.1 tons (5.5 t)

FASTEST SPEED

78 miles (126 km) per hour

CREW

3–4

The U.S. military has thousands of Humvees to quickly move troops and supplies. The first Humvees were made without armor, but today most Humvees have armor.

The armor that covers an armored vehicle is made out of metal and other strong materials. It stops bullets, GRENADES (*greh-NAYDZ*), and other weapons from tearing into the vehicle. The windows of some armored vehicles can stop bullets, too.

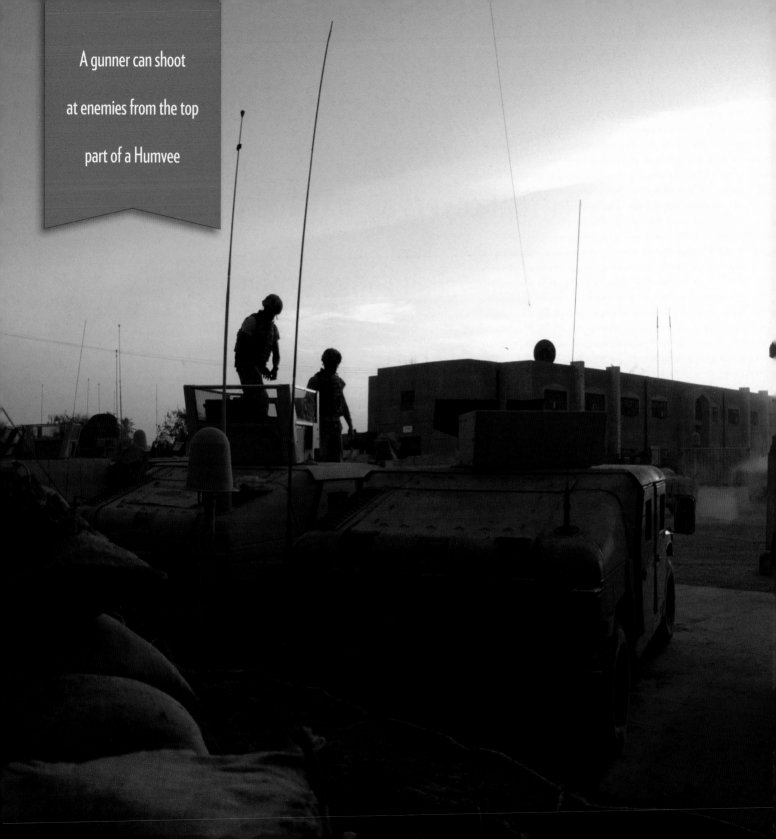

A gunner can shoot
at enemies from the top
part of a Humvee

Most armored vehicles have a crew of two or three soldiers. A driver steers the vehicle. The commander tells the other crew members what to do. A gunner fires the vehicle's weapons. Other troops sit on benches in the back of some armored vehicles.

A battle zone (top);

U.S. soldiers (bottom left);

a tank (bottom right)

When an armored vehicle goes into battle, it carries troops or supplies to where they are needed. The vehicle might stay near troops so they can get inside if the fighting becomes too dangerous. Armored vehicles often travel with tanks.

Most armored vehicles have weapons such as

AUTOMATIC CANNONS and MISSILES (*MIS-sulz*).

The weapons can protect the vehicle and its

soldiers against enemies. They keep the

armored vehicle safe to fight another day!

Stryker

COUNTRY

United States

ENTERED SERVICE

2002

LENGTH

23 feet (7 m)

WIDTH

8.9 feet (2.7 m)

WEIGHT

16.2 tons (14.7 t)

FASTEST SPEED

62 miles (100 km) per hour

CREW

2–3 (plus 9 passengers)

The Stryker's eight wheels can move it quickly over almost any kind of ground, including city streets. It has computers that let troops in one Stryker send messages to troops in another Stryker.

GLOSSARY

armor—a layer of metal and other strong materials that covers a military vehicle and protects it from attacks

automatic cannons—large guns that shoot many bullets very quickly

grenades—small bombs that soldiers can throw with their hands or shoot from guns

missiles—exploding weapons that are pushed through the air by rockets to hit a target

tracks—metal and rubber belts that loop around the wheels of some vehicles to move them over the ground

troops—soldiers or other people who fight in a war

INDEX

ambulances 6

armor 6, 9, 16, 17

crews 10, 16, 19, 23

Humvee 16

Sd Kfz 251 10

size 10, 13, 16, 23

Stryker 23

tanks 9, 21

tracks 10, 14

troops 6, 21

trucks 6, 9, 13

weapons 19, 22

WEB SITES

Army Info Site: HMMWV Hummer

http://www.us-army-info.com/pages/pics/hummer.html

See pictures of Humvees (also called Hummers) in action.

Super Coloring: Military Coloring Pages

http://www.supercoloring.com/pages/category/military/

Print and color pictures of all your favorite military machines.

READ MORE

David, Jack. *Humvees*. Minneapolis: Torque Books, 2009.

Demarest, Chris. *Alpha, Bravo, Charlie: The Military Alphabet*. New York: Margaret K. McElderry Books, 2005.